APRIL BLAKELY

Good Year Books

An Imprint of Addison-Wesley Educational Publishers, Inc.

Dedication

For Carolyn — Sister, friend, and teacher.
Your spirit lives on in the lives of those you've touched.

Good Year Books

are available for most basic curriculum subjects plus many enrichment areas. For more Good Year Books, contact your local bookseller or educational dealer. For a complete catalog with information about other Good Year Books, please write:

Good Year Books
1900 East Lake Avenue
Glenview, IL 60025

Printed in the United States of America.

ISBN 0-673-36318-X
4 5 6 7 8 9 - MH - 04 03 02 01 00 99

Design: *Meyers Design.*
Illustrator: *Jack Dickason.*

Table of Contents

Preface

Dear Teachers and Parents,

The ability to analyze and solve problems is a critical skill for middle school students. The activities within this book were designed to provide an opportunity to develop and enhance these skills. Each problem has been carefully correlated to meet the standards set by the National Council of Teachers of Mathematics (NCTM). Every problem in MATH BRAINTEASERS builds students' problem-solving skills as they work to solve challenging exercises. Teachers and parents will find this book a welcome addition to their lessons.

At first, some of the solutions in MATH BRAINTEASERS may appear obvious, but upon reflection you will find that the answers are not always simple. I suggest that you discuss each problem as it is completed and review the thought processes involved in solving each exercise. There are four critical steps in solving any problem:

1. **Understand the problem.**
   What do you know?
   What do you need to find out?

Frequently, mistakes are made before any actual calculations begin. Always read carefully what the problem is asking and in what method the answer is expected. For example, an exercise might be written using seconds in its computations but require that the answer be given in minutes or hours. Therefore, any answer given in seconds would be incorrect. Also, remember that not carefully reviewing phrases such as *more than, less than, which one,* and *how many* can lead to incorrect conclusions. Circling the question on your paper is usually helpful.

2. **Plan a strategy.**
   What can you do?

Decide what information you need to solve the problem and organize it. Charts or lists are very helpful at this point because they help to sort the data into usable information. For example, read the problem below.

David spent $17 on school supplies and $5 on video games. Carl spent $9 on school supplies and $18 on video games. How much more did Carl spend than David?

You might simply write:

David — $17 supplies	Carl — $ 9 supplies
$ 5 games	$18 games

3. **Carry out your plan.**
Use the information you gathered to find a solution. There are several strategies to help.

a. Draw a diagram
b. Draw a table
c. Make a list
d. Find a pattern
e. Estimate
f. Guess and test
g. Use algebraic equations
h. Compare with a simpler problem

4. **Reflect on your answer.**
Have you answered the question?
Does your answer seem reasonable?

Decide whether the answer is logical. If so, then congratulations! You have probably solved the problem successfully. If not, then look back to the first three steps. Does each step precisely lead to the next? Look for an error in your logic and try again.

Each exercise in Math Brainteasers is correlated to a Scope and Sequence chart on page vi that will help you organize your lessons. As an extension, we've provided students with space on many pages, where they can creatively write similar problems. You'll also find detailed instructions offering possible solutions for solving each problem in the answer key at the end of this book. These problems could easily be used as five minute time fillers or to build an entire lesson around. At home, you might find that the entire family enjoys them.

Most importantly, whether you're at home or school, remember—make it fun!

Sincerely,

April Blakely
Middle School Math Teacher

Scope and Sequence

NAME ______________________

DATE ______________________

The Hole Story

1. Find the area of the figure.

2. Find the area of the shaded region.

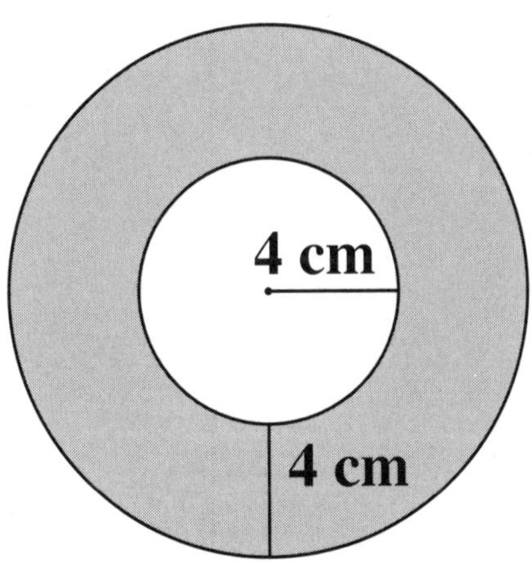

NAME ______________________

DATE ______________________

Mad Math

What is the least number that leaves a remainder of 3 when divided by 5, a remainder of 2 when divided by 4, a remainder of 1 when divided by 3, and a remainder of 0 when divided by 2?

NAME ______________________

DATE ______________________

Rrribbit...

A frog is at the bottom of a $10\frac{1}{2}$ meter well. Each day the frog jumps up 3 meters, but at night it slips down 2 meters. How many days will it take the frog to get out of the well?

NAME ______________________

DATE ______________________

No Bones About It

Jane goes to the grocery store to buy bones for her dog. The butcher tells her that bones come in 3-pound packages for $4.50 or in 5-pound packages for $6.58. Jane wants at least 17 pounds of bones. How many packages of each size should she purchase to get the best buy?

NAME ________________________

DATE ________________________

Follow the Bouncing Ball

A ball rebounds $\frac{1}{2}$ of the height from which it is dropped. Assume the ball is dropped 128 feet from the top of a school and keeps bouncing. How far will the ball have traveled up and down when it strikes the ground for the fifth time?

NAME ______________________

DATE ______________________

More Mad Math

Each letter stands for a different digit. There are 25 possible solutions; how many can you find?

$$
\begin{array}{r}
DOG \\
+\,CAT \\
\hline
TOAD
\end{array}
$$

NAME ______________________

DATE ______________________

Workout

A marathon runner decides to take her dog with her for her daily 20-mile workout. The woman ran at a pace of 10 miles per hour. However, the dog tired after several miles and had to rest frequently. It only managed a pace of 6 miles per hour. How long did the marathoner run? How long did the dog run?

NAME ______________________

DATE ______________________

Boxed In

Place the digits 1 through 9 in the spaces so that each side of the triangle equals 19.

NAME ______________________

DATE ______________________

Mystery Number

1. Find the mystery number. If you multiply it by 1, then add 5, and finally subtract 2, you get 3. What is the mystery number?

2. Find the mystery number. If you multiply it by 3, then subtract 5, and finally add 10, you get 20. What is the mystery number?

NAME

DATE

Voyage to Mars

It takes 15 minutes to travel from Earth to Mars on Interstellar Air Shuttle. The speed of the ship doubles every minute. If the shuttle is traveling at 1,012 miles per minute when it reaches Mars, how many minutes into the trip was the shuttle traveling at a speed of 606 miles per minute?

NAME

DATE

Book Bazaar

Susan bought 10 books at a bazaar. She paid \$2 each for some and \$3 each for the rest of the books. How many \$2 books did Susan buy if she spent \$26?

NAME ______________________________

DATE ______________________________

Roo Race

Two kangaroos decide to have a race. The course was 24 yards long one way, and they race down and back for a total of 48 yards. They both start at the signal "go" and the larger one covers 4 feet per jump while the smaller one covers 2 feet per jump. However, the smaller kangaroo takes two jumps for every jump the larger kangaroo takes. Which kangaroo wins the race and why?

NAME ____________________

DATE ____________________

Hand to Hand

1. If there are 5 people at the party and each person shakes hands with everyone there, how many handshakes are there? (Don't shake your own hand.)

2. If there are 20 people at the party, how many handshakes are there?

NAME ______________________

DATE ______________________

House Hunting

The Martins are looking for a new house. They decide that their new house must have an area of 2,000 square feet. A real estate agent thinks she's found the perfect house, but she doesn't know the exact area. She tells the Martins that the house is shaped like a rectangle with its length being twice its width. Its perimeter is 240 feet. Is the house big enough for the Martins? What is the area of the house?

NAME ______________________

DATE ______________________

Finals

1. Ms. Reynolds, the math teacher, was disappointed to announce that only 22% of her 68 students passed an exam. How many students failed the test?

2. After reviewing the material, Ms. Reynolds retested her class with more positive results. Of the 68 students tested, 75% passed and 12% of those made A's. How many of her students made an A on the exam?

NAME ______________________

DATE ______________________

Farmer Goes to Market

An apple farmer went to town to sell a truck full of apples. At his first stop, he sold $\frac{1}{3}$ of his apples. On the way to the next stop, he wrecked his truck and lost $\frac{1}{3}$ of the remaining apples. Of those he had left, the farmer gave away $\frac{1}{2}$ to some children. He then had 80 apples left. How many apples did the farmer have when he started his trip?

NAME ____________________

DATE ____________________

Shape Shifter

How many triangles can you find?

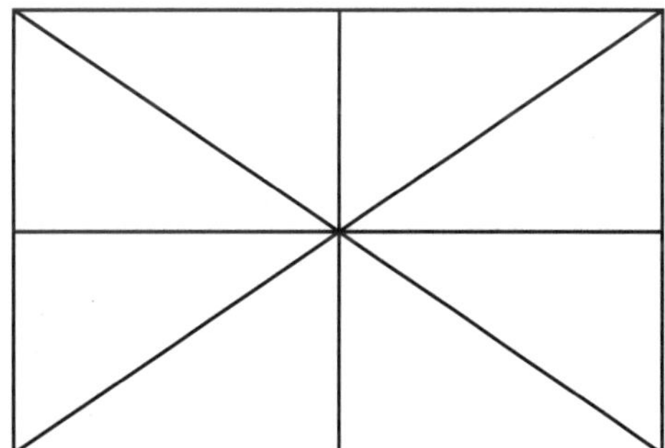

NAME ______________________

DATE ______________________

Jellybeans

Ms. McKee wants to give each student in her class some candy. She wants everyone to receive an equal number of jellybeans. She has less than 100 jellybeans. If she makes groups of 2, 3, or 4 she will have 1 jellybean left over. If she makes groups of 5, she will have no jellybeans left over. How many jellybeans could she have?

NAME ______________________

DATE ______________________

Fraction Action

Mr. Rosette wants all of the employees in his pizza parlor to be good with fractions. Before he hires a new employee, he gives them this test:

Use the numbers in the box to make as many groups of equal fractions as you can. You may use each number as many times as you wish, but the fractions cannot be improper.

1 2 3 4 5 6

How many fractions can you find?

NAME ______________________

DATE ______________________

Bell Ringer

A bell chimes once at 1 o'clock, twice at 2 o'clock, three times at 3 o'clock, and so on. How many times does it chime each day?

NAME ______________________

DATE ______________________

Pascal's Triangle

1. Find the missing numbers.

					1					
				1		1				
			1		2		1			
		1		3		3		1		
	1		4		6		4		1	
___		___		___		___		___		___

2. Extend the triangle by adding five more rows.

NAME

DATE

Soupy Situation

If the can on the left holds 10.75 ounces of chicken soup, how much does the can on the right hold?

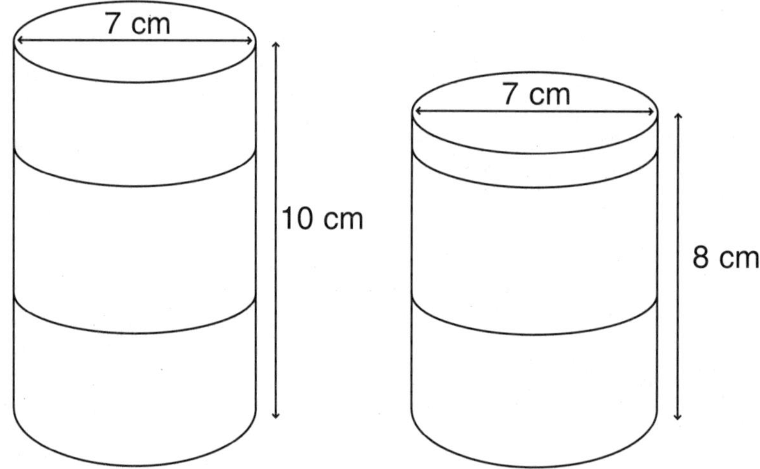

NAME ______________________

DATE ______________________

All Mixed Up

Arrange these numbers in order, from least to greatest.

1. π $\quad 3 \quad \sqrt{3} \quad -3$

2. $2^2 \quad \pi \quad -2 \quad \frac{2}{4}$

3. $\sqrt{4.5} \quad 3^2 \quad \frac{\pi}{3} \quad 3^1$

NAME ______________________

DATE ______________________

Table, Please?

What is the greatest number of tables that you could use to serve dinner to 55 guests so that each table has a different number of guests?

NAME ______________________

DATE ______________________

Show Biz

In rehearsal for a school play, the director estimated a certain number of hours of practice was essential. She calculated that by rehearsing 60 hours per week the play would be ready 1 week earlier than the opening date, but by practicing 40 hours per week it would not be ready until 1 week after the opening date. How many hours per week of rehearsal are necessary for the play to be ready on time?

NAME ______________________

DATE ______________________

Missing Numbers

Fill in the numbers that complete these patterns.

1. 1.25 2 ____ 3.50 ____ ____

   $\frac{1}{2}$ $1\frac{1}{4}$ ____ $2\frac{3}{4}$ ____ ____

2. 3.5 3.75 ____ 4.25 ____ ____

   $\frac{1}{2}$ $\frac{3}{4}$ ____ $1\frac{1}{4}$ ____ ____

3. 7.25 9.75 ____ 14.75 ____ ____

   $\frac{1}{2}$ 3 ____ 8 ____ ____

NAME

DATE

Puppy Puzzle

Brandon's pet Labrador retriever just had puppies. There are four black puppies, two golden puppies, and three mixed-color puppies. None of Brandon's friends can decide which puppy they want so Brandon decides to have a drawing. He puts four black marbles, two yellow marbles, and three striped marbles in a bag to represent the colors of the puppies. He tells his friends that the color they pick is the color puppy they get to take home. What is the probability of getting a black puppy? a golden puppy? a mixed-color puppy?

NAME ______________________

DATE ______________________

Who's Who?

Thea, Maria, and Pam are a teacher, a mechanic, and a pilot. None has a job that starts with the same letter as her name. Thea recently had her car repaired by the mechanic. Who has which job?

Number Perfect

Use the digits 1 through 6 to fill in the circles. The sum of the three numbers on each side of the triangle must be the same. There are 12 possible solutions. How many can you find?

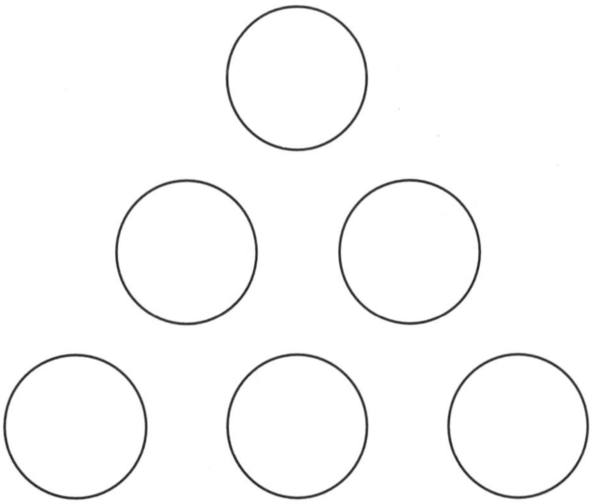

NAME ______________________

DATE ______________________

Fill the Bucket

1. Jill has 4 pints of water in a 4-pint bucket. Jack has an empty 1-pint bucket and an empty 3-pint bucket. None of the buckets has measurement markings. How can they divide the water so each has exactly 2 pints?

2. Jill has 8 pints of water in an 8-pint bucket. Jack has an empty 3-pint bucket and an empty 5-pint bucket. None of the buckets has measurement markings. How can they divide the water so each has exactly 4 pints?

NAME ______________________________

DATE ______________________________

Eating Habits

During a recent school survey of two middle school classrooms, $\frac{1}{3}$ of the students reported that they bring their lunch to school. Another $\frac{1}{4}$ reported that they buy their lunch in the cafeteria and $\frac{1}{6}$ reported going home for lunch. The remaining 18 students reported that they don't eat lunch. How many students are in the two classes?

NAME ______________________

DATE ______________________

Follow the Dots

Use the drawing to complete the number series.

```
*    *    *    *
     **   **   **
          ***  ***
               ****
```

1, 3, 6, 10, ____, ____, ____, ____

NAME ______________________

DATE ______________________

All Gassed Up

When the mechanic at a car dealership checked the cars on the lot, he found that some were $\frac{1}{2}$ full of gas and some were $\frac{1}{4}$ full. There were a total of 85 cars but only enough gas to fill 30 tanks. All of the cars have the same size gas tank. How many cars were $\frac{1}{2}$ full?

NAME ______________________

DATE ______________________

Circle Divide

1. Using only 3 straight lines, divide the circle into 6 pieces.

2. Using only 4 straight lines, divide the circle into 11 pieces.

NAME ______________________

DATE ______________________

Dish Duty

Jenny does the dishes every third day, Mark every fourth day, and Misty every sixth day. If they all shared dish duty today, when will they all share dish duty again?

NAME ______________________

DATE ______________________

The Indy 500

A race car driver completes 360 laps on a $\frac{3}{4}$ mile track in 2 hours. How fast is he driving?

NAME ______________________

DATE ______________________

Abandon Ship!

The passengers of a cruise ship were shocked to learn that their ship was sinking. The ship is 218 feet tall and is sinking at a rate of $\frac{1}{2}$ foot per minute. How long do the passengers have to abandon ship?

NAME

DATE

Going to the Fair

As a special promotion, every 6th person who went to the county fair was given free admission. If a total of 282 people attended, what percentage was admitted free?

NAME ______________________

DATE ______________________

Fruit Fun

A friend gives you three boxes of fruit. One box contains oranges, one contains apples, and one contains both oranges and apples. Unfortunately, your friend has labeled all three boxes incorrectly. Make a plan to relabel the boxes. You may only open one box!

NAME

DATE

Counting Squares

How many squares are in this figure?

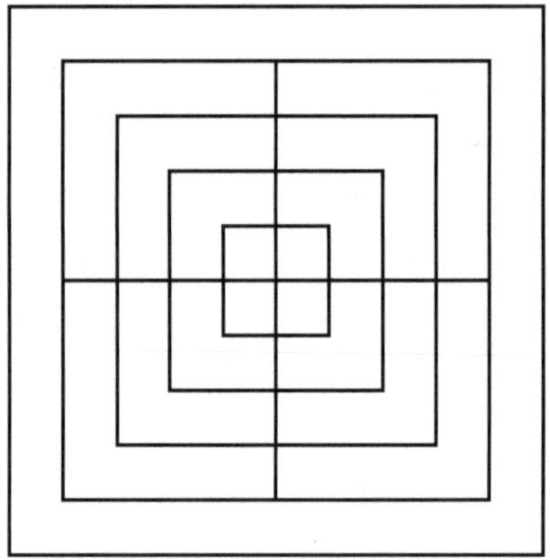

NAME ______________________

DATE ______________________

Holding Hands

There are five groups of three people each holding hands to form a line of people as pictured below.

P-P-P   P-P-P   P-P-P   P-P-P   P-P-P

What is the fewest number of people who must release hands and then rejoin to make one line of 15 people all holding hands?

NAME ______________________

DATE ______________________

Numbers, Please!

There are four numbers. All the numbers are multiples of 5. All are odd numbers. Their sum is 80. What are the numbers?

NAME ______________________

DATE ______________________

Decisions, Decisions

1. Miguel has a difficult choice for lunch. He may have soup or salad; milk or juice; and cake or pie. How many lunch combinations can he choose from?

2. Charmaine can't decide what to wear to a party. She needs to decide between red or blue pants; a white or black shirt; sandals or tennis shoes; and a hat or a hair clip. How many different outfit combinations can she choose from?

NAME ______________________

DATE ______________________

Count a Cube

What is the sum of the number of corners, the number of edges, and the number of sides

1. on a cube?

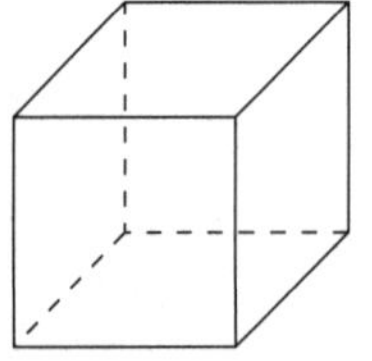

2. on a triangle-based pyramid?

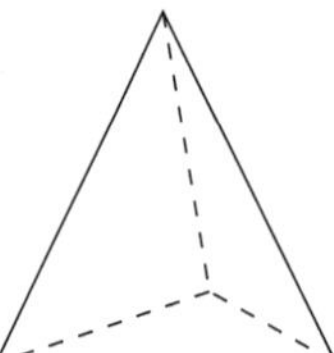

3. on a triangular prism?

4. on a rectangular prism?

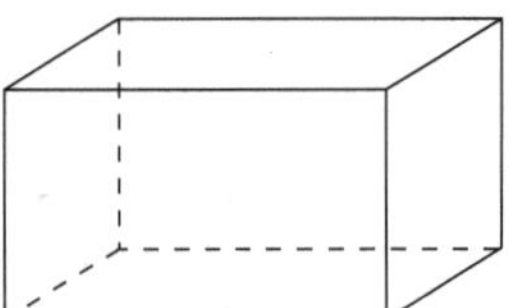

NAME ___________________________

DATE ___________________________

Eggy Situation

The number of eggs in a pound cake is the same as the number of prime numbers less than 10. How many eggs are in the cake?

NAME ____________________

DATE ____________________

Race Day

The winner of a 26-mile marathon averaged a speed of 1 mile every 6 minutes. How much longer did it take the 50th finisher to complete the race if he or she ran at a speed of one mile in $6\frac{1}{2}$ minutes?

NAME ____________________

DATE ____________________

Eggs-actly

Place a dozen eggs in a 6-by-6 carton so that no more than 2 eggs appear in any row either horizontally, vertically, or diagonally.

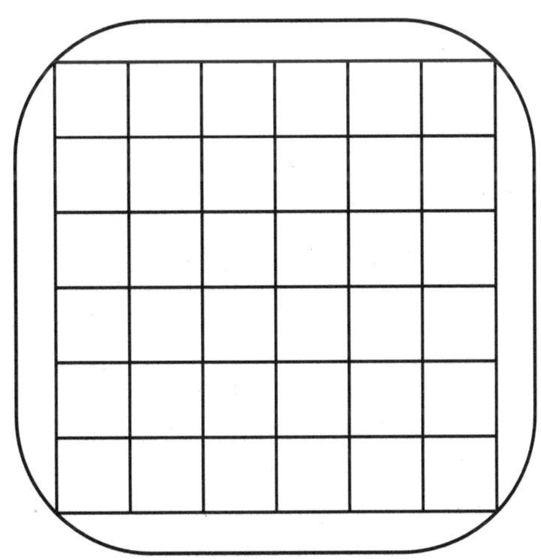

NAME

DATE

Countdown

A man standing in a field to watch the Space Shuttle launch observed that there was a 5-second delay between the blastoff time and the time when he actually heard the sound of the rockets. If sound travels at a speed of 1088 feet per second, how many miles from the launch site was the man?

NAME ______________________

DATE ______________________

Plant a Tree

The Kingston Parks and Recreation Department is planning a new park that will be 100 yards long and 85 yards wide. The department recommended that trees be planted along the perimeter of the park at equal distances from each other and as far apart as possible. How far apart can the trees be planted?

NAME ____________________

DATE ____________________

On and Off

1. A plane departs from an airport. At its first stop, $\frac{1}{2}$ of the passengers leave the plane and 10 new passengers board. There are now 124 passengers on board the plane. How many passengers began the trip? How many are left at the first stop?

2. A certain number of passengers board a cruise ship in Miami. When the ship reaches Jamaica, $\frac{1}{2}$ of the passengers leave the ship and 40 new passengers board. At the Bahamas port, $\frac{1}{4}$ of the passengers leave and 52 new ones board. When the ship reaches Bermuda, $\frac{1}{5}$ leave and 35 board. There are now 163 passengers on board the ship. How many passengers began the cruise in Miami?

NAME ______________________

DATE ______________________

All Boxed Up

A large box is 150 cm long, 57 cm wide, and 54 cm high. Small boxes are 50 cm long, 19 cm wide, and 18 cm high. How many small boxes will fit inside the large box?

NAME ______________________

DATE ______________________

Family Matters

The Johnson family has three sons, Billy, Tommy, and Bobby. Billy is as old as Tommy and Bobby together. Last year, Tommy was twice as old as Bobby was. In two years, Billy will be twice as old as Tommy is now. How old is each son?

NAME ______________________

DATE ______________________

Yard Work

Lana is mowing a lawn 20 feet wide and 80 feet long. The lawnmower blade is 2 feet wide. If Lana starts mowing at an outside corner and continues around the yard without stopping, how far will she have walked when the yard is mowed?

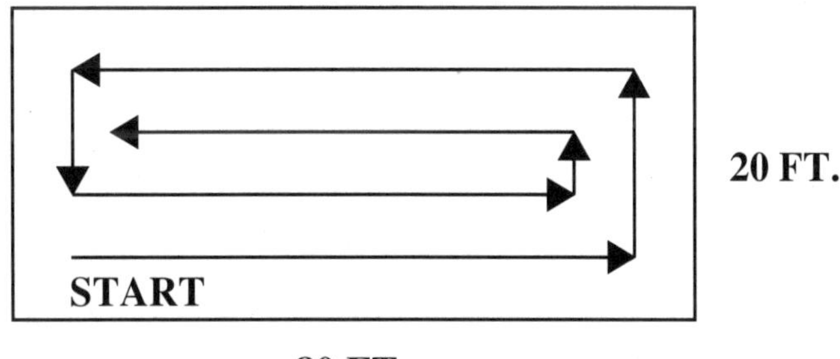

NAME ___

DATE ___

Select a Sign

Group the digits by adding operational signs and parentheses to make a true statement.

1 2 3 4 5 6 7 8 9 = 100

NAME

DATE

Absentminded

Tracy lives 12 miles from her office. On the way to work one morning, she drove 4 miles, then realized that she had forgotten her briefcase. Tracy went home to get it and then drove to work. How many miles did Tracy drive to get to work and home again that day?

NAME ______________________

DATE ______________________

Choices

1. José needs to choose a new number for his locker combination. He can choose any four-digit number using the digits from 1 to 9. How many choices does he have?

2. How many choices would José have if he could use a digit only one time?

NAME ______________________

DATE ______________________

Flower Power

Todd has indigo, yellow, pink, and red flowers in his greenhouse. The ratio of indigo flowers to yellow is 3 to 5. The ratio of yellow to pink is 2 to 4. The ratio of indigo flowers to red is 2 to 5. There are 6 indigo flowers. How many flowers of each color is Todd growing?

NAME ______________________________

DATE ______________________________

Coin Toss

1. A coin is tossed three times. What is the probability of getting heads, heads, and tails?

2. If a coin were tossed three times by three different people, what is the probability of all three people getting heads, heads, and tails?

3. What is the probability that a coin flipped five times will land on heads all five times?

NAME ______________________

DATE ______________________

Space to Roam

A dog is tied to the corner of a house. His leash is 30 feet long. Over how much area can the dog roam?

NAME

DATE

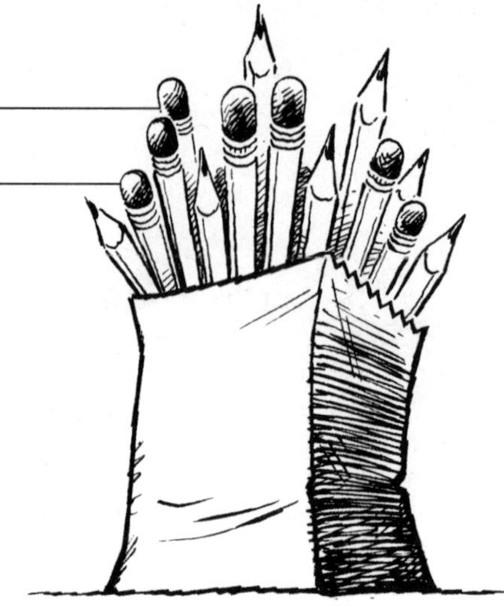

Pencil Probability

1. There are 4 red pencils, 4 blue pencils, and 3 yellow pencils in a bag. A pencil is picked from the bag and then put back. A second pencil is picked. What is the probability that the first pencil is yellow and the second blue?

2. What is the probability that both pencils will be red?

3. What is the probability that the first is blue and the second red?

NAME ______________________

DATE ______________________

Cut the Cube

A cube, painted green on the outside and measuring 15 centimeters on each edge, is cut into congruent cubes measuring 5 centimeters on each edge. How many of the small cubes will have 0 green sides? 1 green side? 2 green sides? 3 green sides?

NAME

DATE

Boxed in Again

Place the digits 1 through 9 in the squares so that each row horizontally, vertically, and diagonally equals 15. (Hint: Place the digit 5 in the center square.)

NAME ______________________

DATE ______________________

Circle in a Square

1. Aunt Martha wants to make a round cake but she only has a square pan. She decides to bake the cake in the square pan and cut it into a round cake after it bakes. What is the radius of the largest circle that can be cut inside a 10-inch square baking pan?

2. At Easter, Aunt Martha decides to make a bunny cake. If she uses her square pan and cuts out round cake sections, how many squares must she bake to create the bunny below?

NAME

DATE

Mail Mistake

Mr. Edwards went to the post office and mailed 7 bills, 3 letters, and 6 cards. After he had deposited the mail in the postal box, Mr. Edwards realized that he had forgotten to put a stamp on one of the envelopes. What is the probability that the unstamped envelope was a bill?

NAME ______________________

DATE ______________________

Slip of the Eye

1. How many squares are there altogether in this diagram?

2. How many triangles are there?

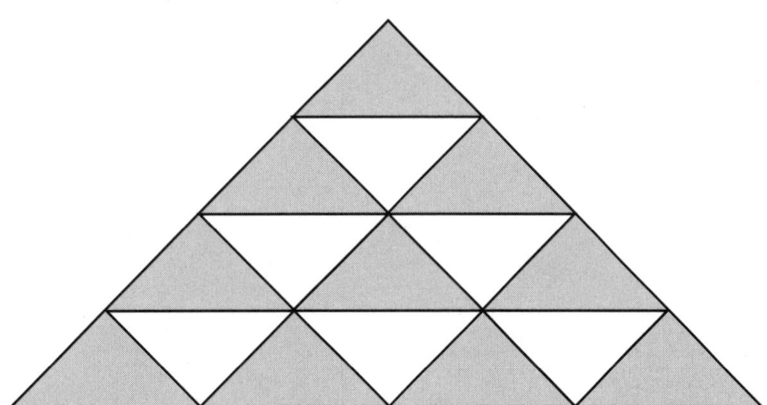

NAME ______________________

DATE ______________________

Pay Raise

Suzanne manages a bookstore and earns $23,500 per year. This amount is $2,500 more than twice as much as she earned when she first started working at the store 9 years ago. How much did she earn when she first started working?

NAME ______________________

DATE ______________________

Travel Time

Martindale and Sunnyvale are 550 miles apart. The Trentons drive from Martindale towards Sunnyvale at 55 mph. The Beldsoes drive from Sunnyvale towards Martindale at 60 mph. How far apart are they after 3 hours?

NAME ______________________

DATE ______________________

Where's the Fire?

A fire truck holds 35,000 gallons of water. If the water is pumped out at a rate of 55 gallons per minute, how long (in hours and minutes) will it take to empty the truck?

NAME ______________________

DATE ______________________

Side by Side

Brandon's and Eric's lockers at school are side by side. The product of their locker numbers is 812. What are the two locker numbers?

NAME ______________________________

DATE ______________________________

Memory Loss

1. Marie went to the store to purchase candy for a party. Unfortunately, she forgot how many pieces of candy her mother said to buy. Marie knows she has exactly the right amount of money if she chooses the correct amount of candy. If the candy costs 6 cents a piece and Marie has $1.56, how many pieces of candy should she purchase?

2. When a man goes to visit a friend, he realizes he can't remember his friend's apartment number. He does remember that his apartment is on the first floor. However, there are 50 apartments on that floor, numbered 101 through 150. He also knows that the apartment number is an even number and a multiple of 3 and 11. What is the correct apartment number?

NAME ______________________

DATE ______________________

Pass the Pencils

A teacher gives 2 pencils each to some of her students. Had she given them 5 pencils each, it would have taken 27 more pencils. How many students were given pencils?

NAME ____________________

DATE ____________________

What-Nots?

The South What-Not factory workers can make 36 small What-Nots or 14 large What-Nots in 1 hour. The North What-Not factory can produce What-Nots $1\frac{1}{2}$ times faster. How many more large What-Nots can the North factory produce in an 8-hour day than the South What-Not factory?

NAME ______________________

DATE ______________________

Five

1. Write the numbers 1 through 5 using only five 5s. Use any operation sign necessary to find the answers, including fractions. The number 1 is done to get you started.

$$1 = \frac{5+5}{5} - \frac{5}{5}$$

2 =

3 =

4 =

5 =

2. Can you also write the numbers 6, 7, 8, and 10? What would you do first?

NAME ______________________

DATE ______________________

Shaping Up

The shaded square has an area of 35 cm². Assuming that the shaded square is equal in size to the adjoining square, what is the area of the entire drawing?

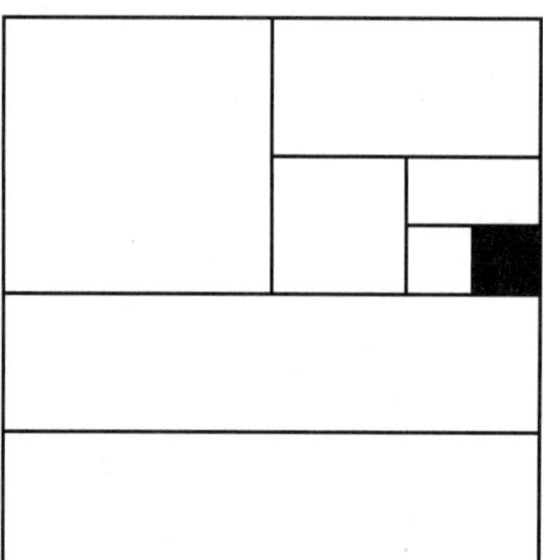

NAME ______________________

DATE ______________________

All Cut Up

How can the figure below be cut into four congruent pieces?

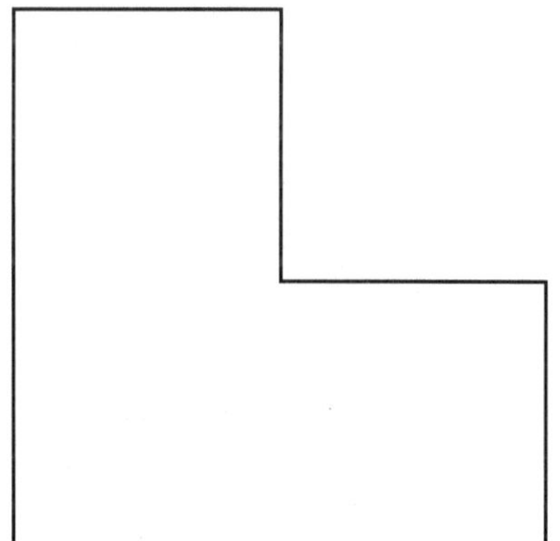

NAME ____________________

DATE ____________________

The Wall

1. The area of a brick wall is 90 m^2. What is its perimeter?

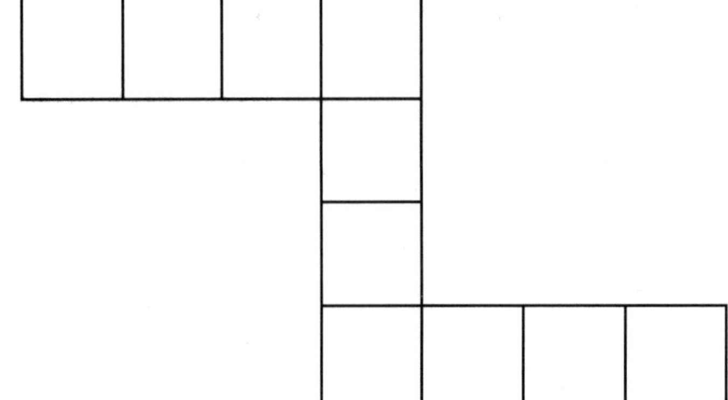

2. If the wall were extended 12 m in each direction, what would the area of the wall be?

NAME ____________________

DATE ____________________

A Tall Tale

1. Jennifer is taller than Autumn but shorter than Tom. Richard's height is between Tom's and Jennifer's. Amy would be the shortest if it were not for Brandon. List the names of the students in order from shortest to tallest.

2. If Jennifer's mom is 90 cm plus half of her own height, how tall is she?

NAME ____________________

DATE ____________________

Treasure Seekers

While searching for sunken treasure in the Atlantic Ocean last year, a treasure hunter found a shipwreck containing many Spanish riches. The gold recovered from the wreck was valued at 6 times the treasure hunter's last find. If his prior discovery was worth 2.34 million dollars, what is the value of his current discovery?

NAME ______________________

DATE ______________________

Punctuality

Josh's watch loses 3.75 seconds every hour. He didn't notice this until he was 18 minutes late for an important meeting one day. How many days has Josh's watch been losing time?

NAME ______________________

DATE ______________________

A Treacherous Ride

A San Francisco streetcar turns curves at the bottom of hills very rapidly. One day a careless driver turned the first of three curves so rapidly that he lost $\frac{1}{2}$ of the passengers. At the second and third curves he again lost $\frac{1}{2}$ of the remaining passengers at each curve. Despite all of this, 8 passengers hung on until the end of the ride. How many passengers started this treacherous streetcar ride?

NAME ______________________

DATE ______________________

The Allowance

After a boy complains for several days about his allowance, his father tells the boy that he will give him a choice. If he agrees to do his chores every day, the father will increase his allowance. However, the boy must choose between two payment plans.

Plan A: $15 per month for one year

or

Plan B: $.01 on the first week, $.02 on the second week, $.04 on the third week, $.08 on the fourth week, $.16 on the fifth week, and so on for one year.

The boy chose Plan A. Why was this a mistake?

NAME ______________________

DATE ______________________

Me and My Shadow

A 6-foot-tall boy is standing next to a telephone pole. If the boy casts a shadow 9 feet long and the telephone pole casts a shadow 42 feet long, about how tall is the telephone pole?

Answer Key

The following instructions describe one possible way to solve each problem. Other problem-solving techniques can be used.

The Hole Story

1) $A = \pi r^2$
   $= 3.14 \times 64$
   $= 200.96 \text{ cm}^2$
2) First, find the area of the large circle:
   $A = \pi r^2$
   $= 3.14 \times 64$
   $= 200.96 \text{ cm}^2$

Then find the area of the small circle:
   $A = \pi r^2$
   $= 3.14 \times 16$
   $= 50.24 \text{ cm}^2$

Subtract the area of the small circle from the area of the large circle to find the area of the shaded region.
   $200.96 - 50.24 = 150.72 \text{ cm}^2$

Mad Math — 58

Working with each clue, students can determine that (1) it is an even number and (2) the last digit is 8. Test numbers 8, 18, 28, 38, etc., to find one that has both a remainder of 2 when divided by 4 and a remainder of 1 when divided by 3.

Rrribbit...

The frog escapes the well on the ninth day. Most students will assume that the answer is 10 days because the frog makes a net gain of 1 meter per day, but they are not considering that once the frog is out of the well on the 9th day it would not fall back that night. Draw a diagram to help.

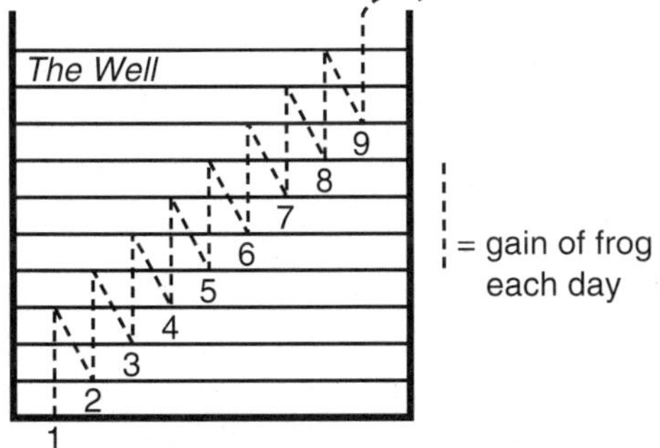

No Bones About It

Four 3-lb. packages plus one 5-lb. package equals 17 lbs. for $24.58. Three 5-lb. packages plus one 3-lb. package equals 18 lbs. for $24.24. Draw a table to organize the data.

3-lb.	Cost	5-lb.	Cost
1	$ 4.50	1	$ 6.58
2	9.00	2	13.16
3	13.50	3	19.74
4	18.00	4	26.32
5	22.50	5	32.90

Follow the Bouncing Ball — 368 feet

The ball travels 128 feet to the ground then bounces $\frac{1}{2}$ way back up and down to the ground again for another 128 feet. Then it bounces $\frac{1}{2}$ way back up and down again for 64 feet. To complete the fourth strike it will travel 32 feet and to complete the fifth strike it will travel 16 feet. Draw a diagram to help.

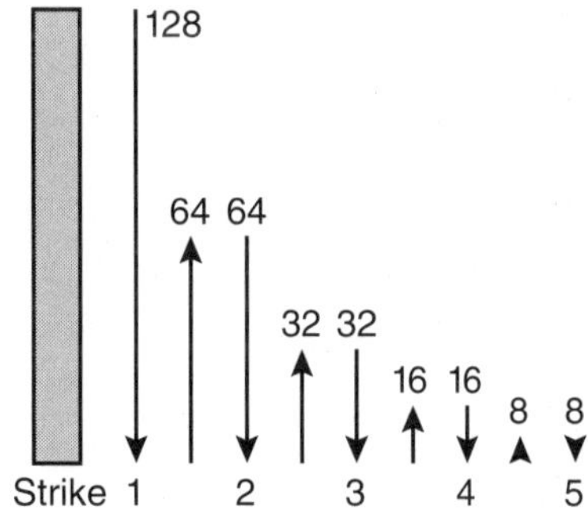

More Mad Math

Some of the possible solutions are:

302	403	605
+741	+621	+421
1,043	1,024	1,026

Solve this problem by finding a pattern. Notice that in the middle column O + A = A. Therefore, O must be equal to zero. Also, T must equal 1 because the largest 3-digit numbers added together would be less than 2,000. Now guess and test to find as many solutions as possible.

Workout
The runner completed his workout in 2 hours ($20 \div 10 = 2$ hours). The dog finishes in 3 hours and 20 minutes ($20 \div 6 = 3.33$).

Boxed In
Numbers may rotate around the triangle, but the 1, 4, and 7 must always be placed in the corners. Begin by making a list of the sets of four numbers that equal 19. Then guess and test for the correct order.

```
         1
      5     8
   9           3
4     2     6     7
```

Mystery Number
Write an algebraic equation. Let a equal the mystery number.
1) $(a \times 1) + 5 - 2 = 3 \quad a = 0$
2) $(a \times 3) - 5 + 10 = 20 \quad a = 5$

Voyage to Mars — 14
If the speed doubles every minute, then 606 miles per minute was achieved at the 14-minute mark.

Book Bazaar — 4
Write an algebraic equation. Let n equal the number of $2 books.
$2n + 3(10 - n) = 26$

Roo Race
The smaller kangaroo wins the race. At the turn the small kangaroo gains the lead because he is able to jump just to the halfway mark and turn. The larger roo must jump past the halfway mark, turn, and start the return toward the finish. This wastes time. During the second half of the race, the small kangaroo is always in the lead. Draw a diagram for visualization.

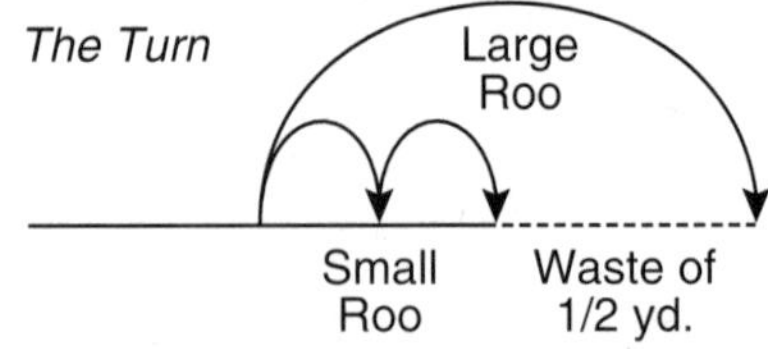

Hand to Hand
Write an algebraic equation. Let x equal the number of handshakes.
1) $\frac{5 \times 4}{2} = 10$ 2) $x = \frac{20 \times 19}{2} = 190$

Divide by 2 because the guests did not shake their own hands.

House Hunting — Yes. 3,200 square feet
Use the perimeter (240) to determine the length of the house (80 feet) and the width (40 feet).
Area = length × width.

Finals
1) First, determine the percent failing (78%), then multiply by the number of students (68). The answer is 53.
2) $68 \times 75\% = 51$ passed; $51 \times 12\% = 6.12$ or 6

Farmer Goes to Market — 360 apples
Write an algebraic equation. Let a equal the number of apples the farmer started with.

$$80 = \tfrac{2}{3}a - \tfrac{1}{3}(\tfrac{2}{3}a) - \tfrac{1}{2}[\tfrac{2}{3}a - \tfrac{1}{3}(\tfrac{2}{3}a)]$$
$$80 = \tfrac{2}{3}a - \tfrac{2}{9}a - \tfrac{1}{3}a + \tfrac{1}{9}a$$
$$80 = \tfrac{2}{9}a$$
$$a = 360$$

Shape Shifter
There are 12 triangles. Draw a diagram to help separate the triangles.

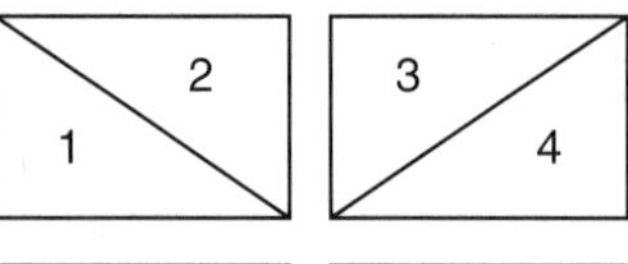

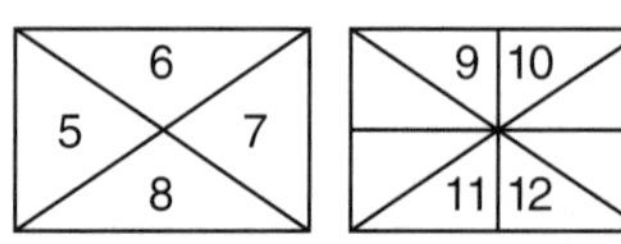

Jellybeans — 85 or 25
The number is a multiple of 5 but not of 2. Therefore, the last digit of the number is a 5. Trial and error testing for a remainder of 1 will eliminate all other numbers.

Fraction Action
$\frac{1}{1}, \frac{2}{2}, \frac{3}{3}, \frac{4}{4}, \frac{5}{5}$, and $\frac{6}{6}$; $\frac{1}{2}, \frac{2}{4}$, and $\frac{3}{6}$; $\frac{1}{3}$ and $\frac{2}{6}$; $\frac{2}{3}$ and $\frac{4}{6}$.

Bell Ringer
During a 24-hour day, the bell will chime 156 times.
$2(1 + 2 + 3 + 4 + 5 + 6 + 7 + 8 + 9 + 10 + 11 + 12) = 156$

Pascal's Triangle

```
1)          1   5   10   10   5   1
2)       1   6   15   20   15   6   1
      1   7   21   35   35   21   7   1
    1   8   28   56   70   56   28   8   1
  1   9   36   84  126  126   84   36   9   1
1   10   45  120  210  252  210  120   45   10   1
```

Look for a pattern. This is Pascal's triangle. Each number, except the first and last number in each row, is the sum of the two numbers above it.

Soupy Situation — 8.6 ounces
Set up a proportion with weight/volume ratios.
Volume of the large can $= \pi r^2 \times h = 384.65$ cm³
Volume of the small can $= 307.72$ cm³

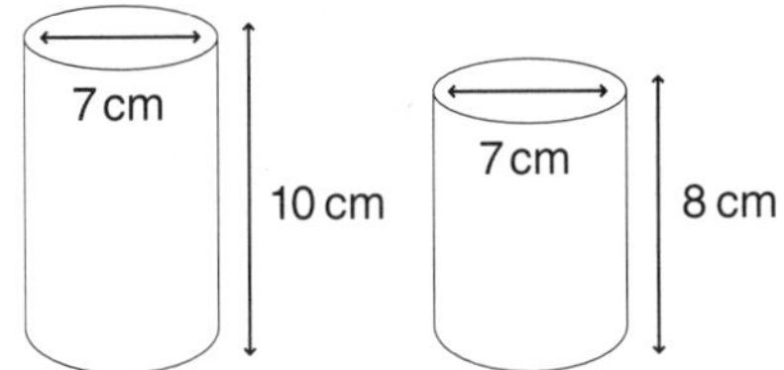

All Mixed Up
1) $-3, \sqrt{3}, 3, \pi$

2) $-2, \frac{2}{4}, \pi, 2^2$

3) $\frac{\pi}{3}, \sqrt{4.5}, 3^1, 3^2$

Simplify the problem by reasoning that:
1) $\pi = 3.14$ and $\sqrt{3} = 1.73$

2) $2^2 = 4$; $\pi = 3.14$; and $\frac{2}{4} = .5$

3) $3^1 = 3$, $3^2 = 9$, $\frac{\pi}{3} < 3$, $\sqrt{4.5} < 3$, and $\frac{\pi}{3} < \sqrt{4.5}$

Table, Please? — 10 tables
For the greatest possible number of tables to be used, each must seat the least possible number of guests.
$(1+2+3+4+5+6+7+8+9+10=55)$

Show Biz
48 hours of rehearsal per week are required for the play to open on time. Write an algebraic equation. Let x equal the number of weeks before the play opens.
$60(x-1) = 40(x+1)$
$x = 5$
$(60 \times 5) - 60 = 240$
$(40 \times 5) + 40 = 240$
$240 \div 5 = 48$

Missing Numbers

1) 2.75, 4.25, 5 (Add .75 each time)
   $2, 3\frac{1}{2}, 4\frac{1}{4}$ (Add $\frac{3}{4}$ each time)
2) 4, 4.5, 4.75 (Add .25 each time)
   $1, 1\frac{1}{2}, 1\frac{3}{4}$ (Add $\frac{1}{4}$ each time)
3) 12.25, 17.25, 19.75 (Add 2.25 each time)
   $5\frac{1}{2}, 10\frac{1}{2}, 13$ (Add $2\frac{1}{2}$ each time)

Puppy Puzzle
Black = 4 out of 9 (44.4%); golden = 2 out of 9 (22.2%); and mixed-color = 3 out of 9 (33.3%). Divide the number of each color by the total number of puppies.

Who's Who?
Thea is the pilot. Maria is the teacher. Pam is the mechanic. Compare the data to conclude in this order: (1) Thea is not the teacher or the mechanic. Thea must be the pilot. (2) Maria is not the mechanic or the pilot. Maria must be the teacher. (3) Pam is not the teacher or the pilot. Pam must be the mechanic.

Number Perfect
Some of the possible solutions are:
Rows equal 9:

    1
  5   6
3   4   2

Rows equal 10:

    5
  4   2
1   6   3

Rows equal 11:

    2
  5   3
4   1   6

Make a list of all the possible combinations of three numbers that add up to 9, 10, 11, etc. Use the sets to guess and test number arrangements until you find combinations that meet the criteria.

Fill the Bucket
Follow these steps:
1) 1. Fill the 3-pint bucket from the 4-pint bucket.
   2. Fill the 1-pint bucket from the 3-pint bucket.
   3. Pour the 1-pint bucket into the 4-pint bucket.
2) 1. Fill the 5-pint bucket from the 8-pint bucket.
   2. Fill the 3-pint bucket from the 5-pint bucket.
   3. Pour the 3-pint bucket into the 8-pint bucket.
   4. Pour the 5-pint bucket into the 3-pint bucket.
   5. Fill the 5-pint bucket from the 8-pint bucket.
   6. Fill the 3-pint bucket from the 5-pint bucket.
   7. Pour the 3-pint bucket into the 8-pint bucket.

Draw a step-by-step diagram for visualization.

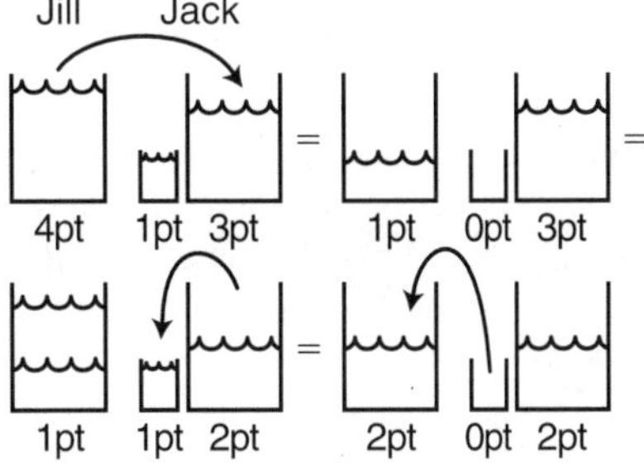

Eating Habits — 72

$\frac{1}{3}+\frac{1}{4}+\frac{1}{6}=\frac{9}{12}$ or $\frac{3}{4}$; therefore, the remaining $18=\frac{1}{4}$;

$18\times4=72$

Follow the Dots — 15, 21, 28, 36

One row with one additional star is added in each drawing.

All Gassed Up

Write an algebraic equation. Let $x=$ # cars $\frac{1}{2}$ full and $85-x=$ # cars $\frac{1}{4}$ full.

$\frac{1}{2}x+\frac{1}{4}(85-x)=30$

$2x+85-x=120$

$x=35$ cars are half full

Circle Divide

Lines may vary.

1) 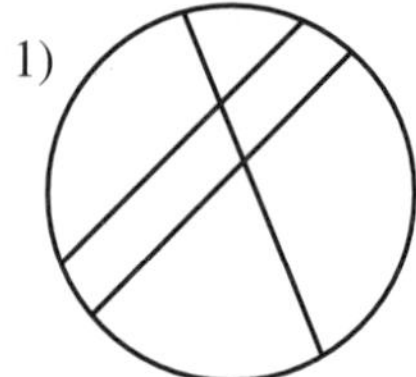

2) 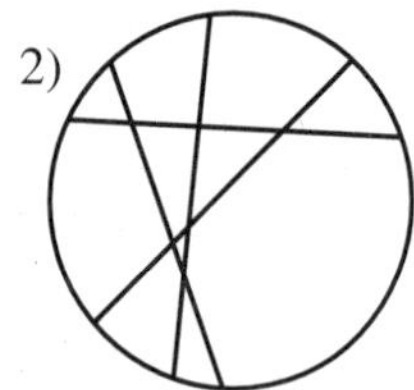

Dish Duty

12 days; 12 is the least common multiple of 3, 4, and 6.

The Indy 500

First, determine how many miles the driver has completed.

$360\times.75=270$

Then divide by 2 hours to determine the miles per hour.

$270\div2=135$ miles per hour

Abandon Ship! — 7 hours and 16 minutes

Write an algebraic equation. Let x equal the minutes until the ship sinks.

$218=\frac{2}{9}x$

$x=436$ minutes

Going to the Fair — 16.67%

$282\div6=47$ persons admitted free

$\frac{47}{282}\times100\%=16.67\%$

Fruit Fun

Open the box marked apples and oranges. If there are oranges inside, then: (1) relabel the box labeled "mixed box" oranges, (2) relabel the box labeled "apples" mixed fruit, and (3) relabel the "orange box" apples. If there are apples inside, then: (1) relabel the "mixed box" apples, (2) relabel the "orange box" mixed fruit, and (3) relabel the "apple box" oranges.

Counting Squares — 21 squares.

Draw a diagram to help separate the squares.

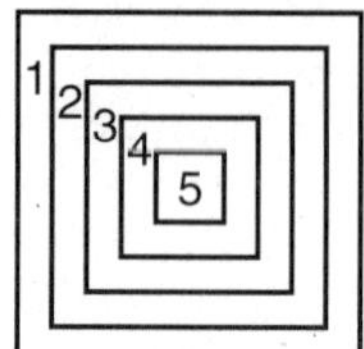

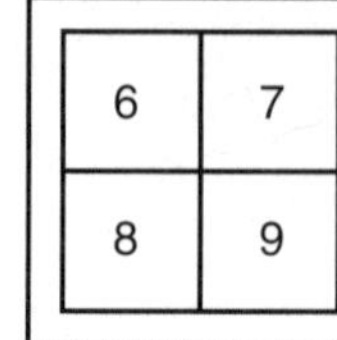

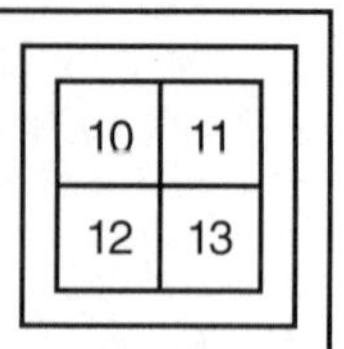

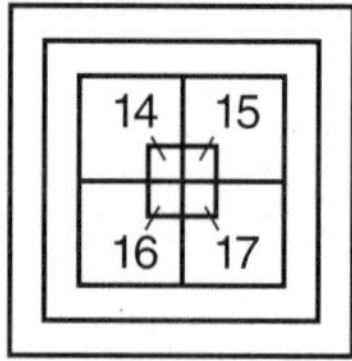

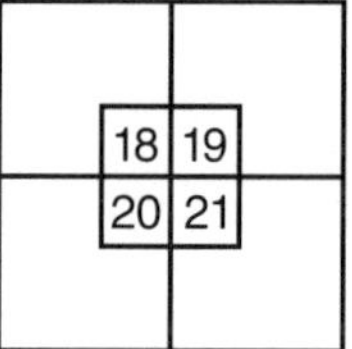

Holding Hands — 3 people.

One of the five groups should separate and those three people place themselves between the other four groups.

Numbers, Please! — 5, 15, 25, 35

Add the first 4 odd multiples of 5 together.

Decisions, Decisions

1) $2\times2\times2=8$ combinations

2) $2\times2\times2\times2=16$ outfits. You may also make a list of the possible combinations.

Count a Cube

1) 26; there are 8 corners, 12 edges, and 6 sides on a cube.

2) $4+6+4=14$

3) $6+9+5=20$

4) $8+12+6=26$

Draw a diagram to help. Guess and test to find the correct arrangement of lines.

Eggy Situation — 4

The prime numbers less than 10 are 2, 3, 5, and 7.

Race Day — 13 minutes

The 50th finisher fell behind by an average of 30 seconds every mile.

$26\times30=780$ seconds or 13 minutes.

Eggs-actly

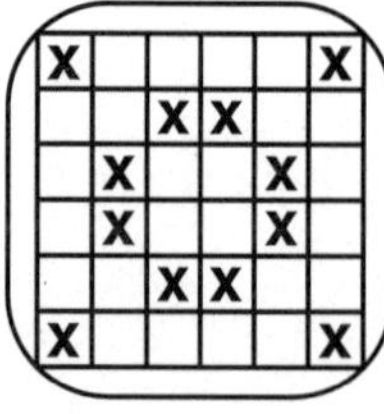

Guess and test to find the correct solution.

Countdown
$1088 \times 5 = 5{,}440$. There are 5,280 feet in one mile; therefore, $5{,}440 \div 5{,}280 = 1.03$ mile.

Plant a Tree — 5 yards
Five is the only common factor of both 85 and 100. Any other arrangement of trees would not be at equal distances. An alternate solution is along the perimeter 185 yards apart, although this is not practical.

On and Off
Work backwards:

1) $124 - 10 + \frac{1}{2} = 228$ passengers began the flight and 114 left.
   Or write an algebraic equation: p = passengers at the start
   $\frac{1}{2}p + 10 = 124$
   $\frac{1}{2}p = 114$
   $p = 228$
2) Let p equal the number of passengers at the start of the trip, giving you 208 passengers who began the cruise.
   $\frac{4}{5}[\frac{3}{4}(\frac{1}{2}p + 40) + 52] + 35 = 163$
   $\frac{4}{5}[\frac{3}{8}p + 30 + 52] = 128$
   $\frac{3}{8}p + 82 = 160$
   $\frac{3}{8}p = 78$
   $p = 208$

All Boxed Up
Determine that 3 small boxes fit along the length, 3 small boxes fit along the width, and 3 small boxes fit along the height of the large box. $3 \times 3 \times 3 = 27$.

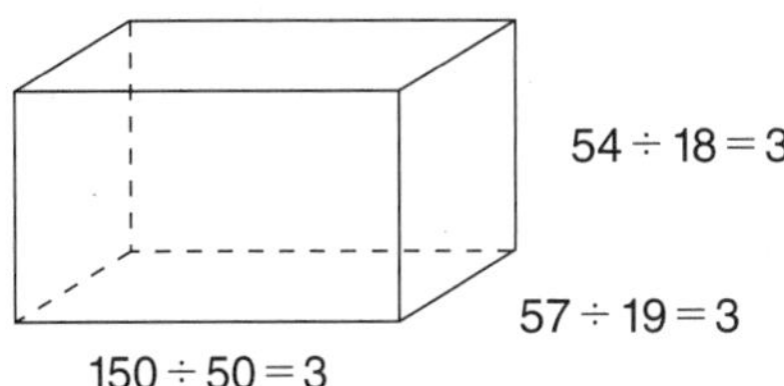

Family Matters
Make a table to sort out the information.
Billy = Tommy + Bobby
Tommy − 1 year = 2 × Bobby − 1 year
Billy + 2 years = 2 × Tommy
Now guess and test for the correct answer. Billy is 8, Tommy is 5, and Bobby is 3.

Yard Work — 840 feet
Each complete pass reduces the distance walked by 16 feet. It will take 5 passes to completely mow the yard.

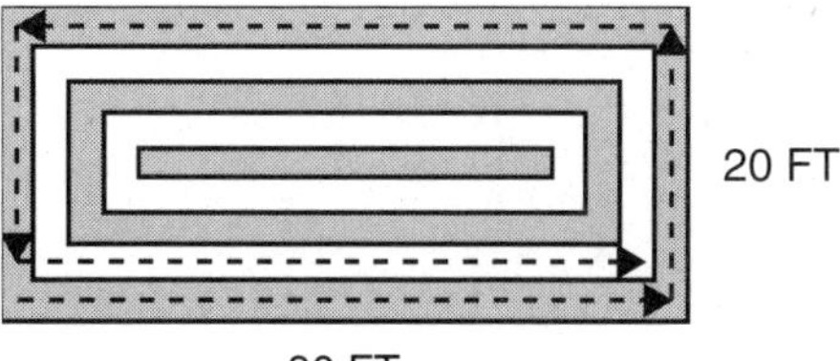

1st pass $= 2(80 + 20) = 200$
2nd pass $= 2(76 + 16) = 184$
3rd pass $= 2(72 + 12) = 168$
4th pass $= 2(68 + 8) = 152$
5th pass $= 2(64 + 4) = 136$
840 feet

Select a Sign
Several solutions are possible.
$1(2 + 3) \times 4 \times 5 - 6 + 7 + 8 - 9 = 100$
$1 + 2 + 3 + 4 + 5 + 6 + 7 + (8 \times 9) = 100$
$(1 + 2 + 3 + 4 + 5) \times 6 - 7 + 8 + 9 = 100$

Absentminded — 32 miles
$4 + 4 + 12 + 12 = 32$
It might be helpful to draw a diagram of the trip.

Choices

1) $9 \times 9 \times 9 \times 9 = 6{,}561$.
2) Formula: (a) (a − 1) (a − 2) (a − 3)
   $9 \times 8 \times 7 \times 6 = 3{,}024$

You may also begin a list to find a pattern.

Flower Power
There are 6 indigo, 10 yellow, 20 pink, and 15 red flowers. Use the known quantity of indigo flowers to set up ratios for the remaining colors. Let n equal yellow, m equal pink, and p equal red.
Indigo to yellow is $\frac{3}{5} = \frac{6}{n}$ $n = 10$
Yellow to pink is $\frac{2}{4} = \frac{10}{m}$ $m = 20$
Indigo to red is $\frac{2}{5} = \frac{6}{p}$ $p = 15$

Coin Toss

1) 1 out of 8 times or 12.5%. There are 8 possible outcomes. Only one is heads, heads, tails. It might be helpful to make a list of the possibilities.

HHH	HHT	HTT	TTT
THH	TTH	THT	HTH

2) 1 out of 512 times or .195%
   $\frac{1}{8} \times \frac{1}{8} \times \frac{1}{8} = \frac{1}{512}$
3) Approximately 3%
   $(\frac{1}{2})(\frac{1}{2})(\frac{1}{2})(\frac{1}{2})(\frac{1}{2}) = \frac{1}{32}$ or .33

Space to Roam
If the dog is tied to a corner, then it may roam in a circle excluding the part of the circle that the house occupies. This would be 90 degrees or $\frac{1}{4}$ of the circle. Find the area of the circle and subtract $\frac{1}{4}$ to determine the area that the dog can roam. Draw a picture for visualization.

$A = \pi \times r^2$

$A = 2826 \text{ ft}^2$

$2{,}826 \times \frac{3}{4} = 2{,}119.5 \text{ ft}^2$

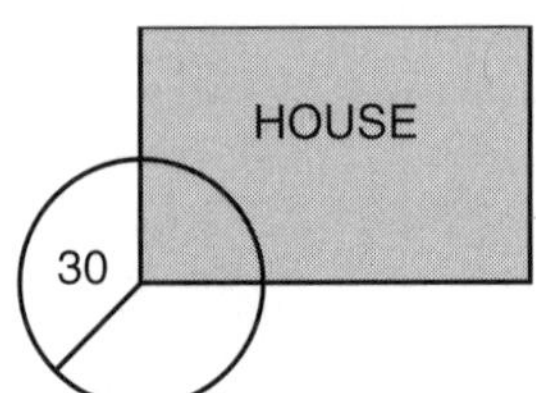

The dog may roam in a 270 degree radius.

Pencil Probability
Write as a ratio to solve. The probability that the draw will be yellow is $\frac{3}{11}$, red is $\frac{4}{11}$, and blue is $\frac{4}{11}$. Therefore, the probability of drawing yellow and then blue can be stated: P (yellow, then blue) = P (yellow) × P (blue)

1) $\frac{3}{11} \times \frac{4}{11} = \frac{12}{121}$ or about 10%
2) $\frac{4}{11} \times \frac{4}{11} = \frac{16}{121}$ or 13%
3) $\frac{4}{11} \times \frac{4}{11} = \frac{16}{121}$ or 13%

Cut the Cube
0 green sides = 1 (the center of large cube); 1 green side = 6 (centers of each side); 2 green sides = 12 (corner center cubes); and 3 green sides = 8 (corner cubes). Draw a diagram to help visualize the cube. There are 27 total cubes.

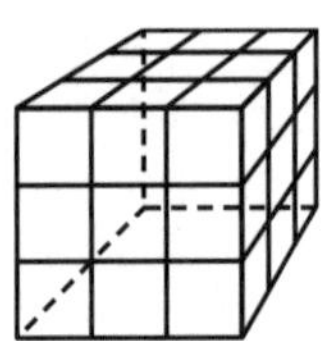

Boxed in Again
This problem is basically guess and test. However, it does help to make a list of all the possible combinations of three numbers that add up to 15. Then look at the sets. Five is used most frequently. It is in four sets and therefore is the only digit that could be placed in the middle box.

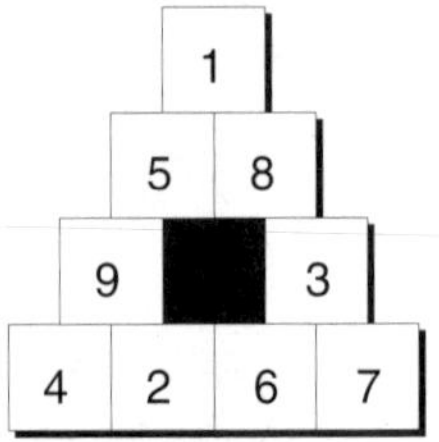

Circle in a Square
1) 5 inches. The diameter of the largest possible circle is the length of one side of the square. The radius is half of the diameter. Draw a diagram for visualization.
2) 2 squares. Face = 1 circle; ears = 1 circle; tie from extra corners of pan.

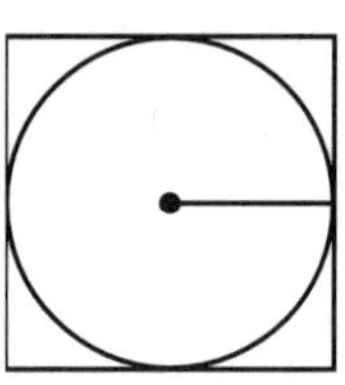

10 in. pan

Mail Mistake
The total number of envelopes mailed was 16. $\frac{7}{16} = .4375$ or 43.75%

Slip of the Eye
7 squares and 26 triangles. Draw a copy of the diagram and mark the triangles or quadrilaterals as you find them. This will prevent you from counting the same shape twice.

Triangles:

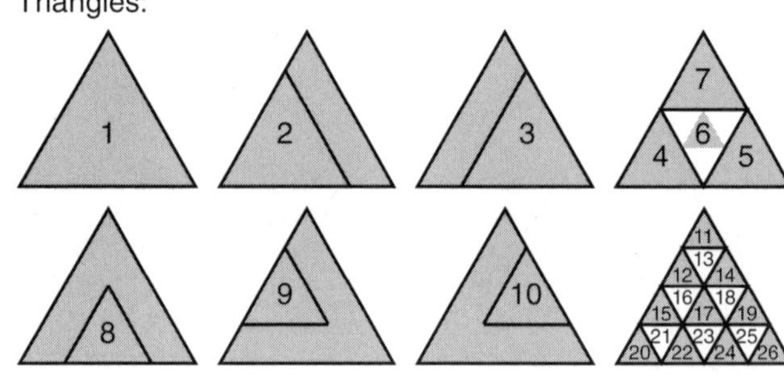

Squares:

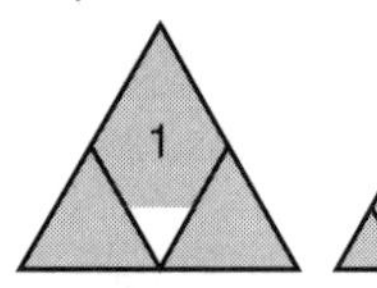

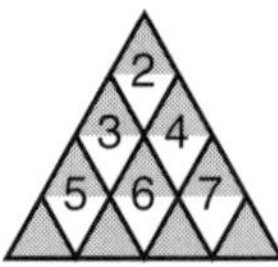

Pay Raise — $10,500
Subtract the increase from her current salary and divide by two. (23,500 − 2,500) ÷ 2 = 10,500

Travel Time
Find the distance traveled by each family and subtract from the total distance.
550 − (55 × 3) − (60 × 3) = 205 miles

Where's the Fire? — 1 hour and 10 minutes
Divide the total gallons of water by the rate per minute then convert to hours and minutes.

35,000 ÷ 500 = 70 minutes

Side by Side — 28 and 29

Write a factor tree for 812. Look for a reasonable combination that, when multiplied, will equal 812. ($7 \times 2 \times 2 = 28$; $28 \times 29 = 812$)

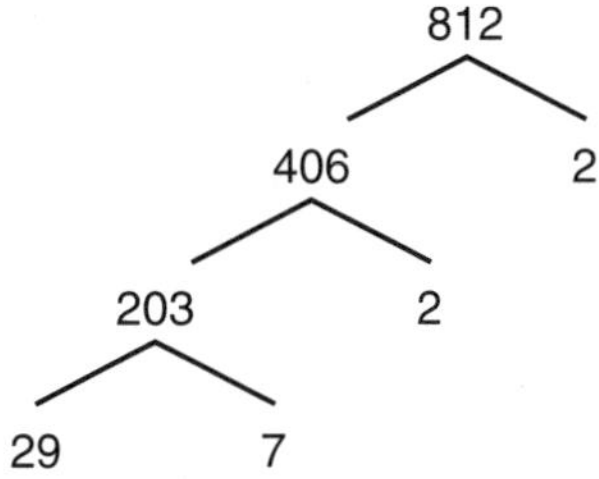

Memory Loss

1) Marie should purchase 26 pieces of candy. \$1.56 divided by 6 equals 26. The number 156 is a multiple of 6.
2) 132. Make a list of the even numbers between 101 and 150 and then guess and test each number to find the multiples of 3 and 11. The only number that is a multiple of both is 132.

Pass the Pencils — 9

The difference between 2 and 5 is 3. ($\frac{27}{3} = 9$)

What-Nots?

Multiply to find the North factory's production for 8 hours.

$14 \times 1\frac{1}{2} = 21$

$21 \times 8 = 168$

Multiply to find the South factory's production for 8 hours.

$14 \times 8 = 112$

Subtract.

$168 - 112 = 56$ more large What-Nots

Five

$2 = \frac{5+5}{5} + (5 - 5)$

$3 = \frac{5+5}{5} + (5 \div 5)$

$4 = \frac{5}{5 \div 5} - \frac{5}{5}$

$5 = \frac{5}{5 \div 5} + (5 - 5)$

Use the answer given for 1 to help you find a pattern.

Shaping Up — 2,240 cm^2

The area of the shaded rectangle is half the area of the adjoining rectangle.

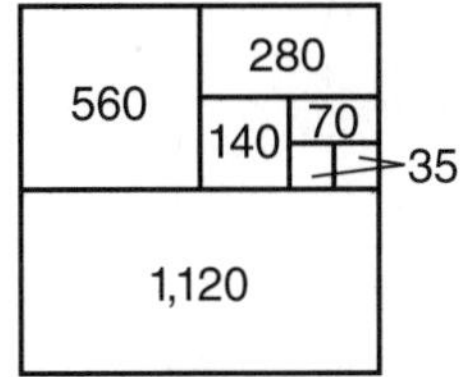

All Cut Up

Remember that congruent figures have the same size and shape. Draw a diagram to guess and test.

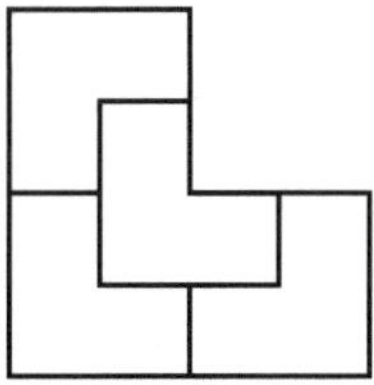

The Wall

1) Divide the total area by the number of bricks to find the area of each stone. $90 \text{ m}^2 \div 10 = 9 \text{ m}^2$ per stone Since the perimeter $= s^2$, each side equals 3 m. The perimeter is 66 m.
2) $18 \times 9 \text{ m}^2 = 162 \text{ m}^2$

A Tall Tale

1) Brandon, Amy, Autumn, Jennifer, Richard, and Tom. Work with the first clue to arrange the first three people, then add in the rest of the people using the second and third clues.
   Step 1: Autumn, Jennifer, Tom
   Step 2: Autumn, Jennifer, Richard, Tom
   Step 3: Brandon, Amy, Autumn, Jennifer, Richard, and Tom
2) 180 cm tall
   Since she is 90 cm plus $\frac{1}{2}$ her own height, 90 cm is $\frac{1}{2}$ her height and the other $\frac{1}{2}$ must also be 90 cm.

Treasure Seekers — 14.04 million dollars

Multiply the value of the prior discovery by 6 to find the value of the current treasure.

Punctuality

First, determine the number of seconds Josh's watch has lost.

18 min. $\times$ 60 seconds per min. = 1080 sec.

Next, divide the seconds lost by the seconds per minute.

$1080 \div 3.75 = 288$ hours or 12 days

A Treacherous Ride — 64

Write an algebraic equation. Let x equal the number of passengers on the streetcar. After the first curve:

$x - \frac{1}{2}x = \frac{1}{2}x$

After the second curve:

$\frac{1}{2}x - \frac{1}{2}(\frac{1}{2}x) = \frac{1}{2}x - \frac{1}{4}$

After the third curve:

$\frac{1}{4}x - \frac{1}{2}(\frac{1}{4}x) = 8$

$\frac{1}{4}x - \frac{1}{8} = 8$

$\frac{1}{8}x = 8$

$x = 64$

The Allowance

Comparing the annual allowances:
Plan A = $180 per year
Plan B = Over a trillion dollars!
Make a table to show how the allowance in Plan B dramatically increases.

Week	Amount
1	.01
2	.02
3	.04
4	.08
5	.16
6	.32
7	.64
8	1.28
↓	↓
20	5242.88
	and so on...

Me and My Shadow

First, find the distance of the boy's shadow per foot.

$6 \div 9 = .66$

Next, multiply the pole's shadow by the boy's shadow.

$42 \times .66 = 27.72$ feet or about 28 feet